Contents

At home

Joe and Christopher Bear are making gooey cakes at home.
"Can you stir as fast as me?" Joe giggles.
Christopher Bear just smiles
his crooked smile, with a
blob of sticky mixture
on his nose.

Dear God, it's fun to make something by myself!
Thank you for people who show me what to do.
Amen.

At preschool

There are so many activities to choose from at preschool! Christopher Bear is helping Joe and Harry to make mountains out of sand.

Dear God, thank you for sand and water, for toys and friends. Thank you for my teachers who look after me. Amen.

Outdoors

Christopher Bear loves swinging with Joe.
"Can you touch the sky with your feet?" asks Joe.

Dear God, thank you for making the big, big sky.
Thank you for friends to play with. And thank you for
your great big wonderful world. Amen.

Indoors

Joe and Christopher Bear have made a big mess today!
They've scribbled on the walls and left toys lying around everywhere.
Mom is helping to tidy up.

Dear God, playing at home with all my things is great
fun. Help me to remember to tidy up too!
Amen.

Special things

Christopher Bear loves whizzing round very fast on the merry-go-round. It makes his tummy feel all fluttery inside, but he feels safe with Joe.

Dear God, thank you for the special things we can do with our friends: the swing, the slide and the merry-go-round. Amen.

Doing favorite things

It's raining outside, but Joe doesn't care.
He loves playing indoors with Christopher Bear!

Thank you, dear God, for my home.
And thank you for my favorite toys.
Amen.

Feeling loved

"Do you love me?" asks Joe. "As much as I love Christopher Bear?"
"Even more than that!" says Mom.

Dear God, thank you for the special people who love me lots! Thank you that you love me too. Amen.

Missing someone

Joe is at preschool, but Christopher Bear is at home today. Joe is missing him. Do you ever miss someone special when you are away from them?

Dear God, when I feel sad and I am missing someone special, please help me to remember that you are always with me. Amen.

Feeling lonely

Joe is sitting all alone today. All his friends are busy and nobody is playing with him. Joe feels sad.

Dear God, sometimes I feel a bit lonely and left out. Thank you that I can always talk to you. Amen.

Ouch! It hurts!

Poor Joe has fallen over with a big bump and hurt his knees. Two large tears roll down his cheeks and splash onto Christopher Bear's fur.

Dear God, thank you that you always care when I get hurt. Thank you for people who help me. Amen.

Can we be friends again?

Joe was really naughty today. He scribbled all over Ben's drawing! Ben was upset about it until Joe said, "I'm sorry." Then they were friends again!

Dear God, I'm sorry when I am mean to my friends. Help me to think how I would feel if they were mean to me and then to be kind. Amen.

I'm sorry

Joe sat on Mom's knee and told her all about being naughty.

"God is sad when we hurt other people," said Mom.

"I said 'I'm sorry' to Ben," said Joe. "Shall I say 'I'm sorry' to God too?"

Dear God, I'm sorry I was naughty today. Thank you that you always love me, whatever I have done. Amen.

It's not fair

Elizabeth won't let Joe play with the cars today. She will only let him have an old yellow one with wonky wheels. "That's not fair!" says Joe.

Dear God, sometimes I feel really cross when things don't seem fair. Help me not to be angry and to forgive other people. Amen.

18

It's mine

Oliver wants to play with Christopher Bear, but Joe won't let him. "He's mine!" shouts Joe and pushes him out of the way.

Dear God, please help me to share my toys with my friends. I'm sorry when I'm selfish and want to keep everything to myself. Amen.

I can't do it

Joe and his friends are making stars at preschool. But Joe is having trouble cutting them out. He's starting to feel upset. "I can't do it, Miss Rosie!" he says. Christopher Bear wants to help too.

Dear God, when I find something very difficult, please help me to keep on trying, and not get cross and sulky. Amen.

In a new place

When Joe first went to preschool, he didn't know any of the other children. He felt a bit wobbly inside. Miss Rosie came and helped him to settle in.

Dear God, it's sometimes a bit scary in a new place. Help me not to feel too frightened! Thank you for being with me wherever I go. Amen.

In the dark

Joe sometimes feels afraid of the dark
at night in his room. He snuggles
under the covers with
Christopher Bear.
"You're my best friend,"
whispers Joe.

Dear God, thank you that you are always awake, even
when it's dark and I'm in bed. Help me not to be
afraid, because you are always with me. Amen.

Thank you for food

Joe is having breakfast with Christopher Bear.
"Eat everything up, please," says Joe.
What do you like best to eat?

Dear God, thank you for all the lovely food you give me to eat. Thank you for all the people who buy food and cook it for me, too. Amen.

Thank you for families

In Joe's family there is Joe, his mom, Christopher Bear and Sooty the cat. "And we're in God's family too," says Mom. "God loves us this much!"

Dear God, thank you for my home and family and all the special people who love me. Amen.

Thank you for Jesus

At preschool Joe and his friends have been learning about Christmas and how Jesus was born in Bethlehem. They have made a manger, added some hay and Ben's baby brother is going to lie in it!

Dear God, thank you for sending Jesus to be born as a baby. Thank you for Christmas and time to be together and all the exciting things we do. Amen.

What do angels look like?

Joe has learned that an angel told Mary she was going to have a baby called Jesus. Then more angels told the shepherds that Jesus had been born. Joe and Christopher Bear try on some angel's wings. "But what do angels really look like?" he asks.

Dear God, thank you for the angel who came to see Mary, and for the angels who told the shepherds that Jesus had been born. Amen.

Friends are fun!

Jessie has come to play at Joe's house this afternoon. They are having great fun in the garden, playing in the sand and squirting each other with the hose pipe!

Dear God, thank you for buckets and spades, laughter and fun, and friends to play with. Amen.

Sharing

Christopher Bear loves playing with the farm set. Jessie is sharing the animals with Joe.

Dear God, thank you for the fun we have when we share even our special things with friends. Amen.

Everyone is special

There are lots of children in Joe's class at preschool. Each one looks different. Jessie has blonde hair in bunches, Jack has black hair, Oliver has red hair, Polly has curly hair. Joe likes all his friends. They are all very special.

Dear God, thank you that you make everyone different. Thank you that everyone is special to you. Amen.

Published in the United States of America by
Abingdon Press, 201 Eighth Avenue South, Nashville,
Tennessee 37203
ISBN 0-687-07585-8

First edition 2003

Copyright © 2003 AD Publishing Services Ltd
1 Churchgates, The Wilderness, Berkhamsted, Herts HP4 2UB
Text copyright © 2003 AD Publishing Services Ltd: Leena Lane
Illustrations copyright © 2003 Jacqui Thomas

Editorial Director Annette Reynolds
Project Editor Leena Lane
Art Director Gerald Rogers
Pre-production Krystyna Hewitt
Production John Laister

Printed and bound in Singapore

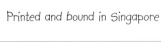